STECK-VAUGHN BOLDPRINT®

Galaxies Await

ROBERT CUTTING

Steck-Vaughn®

HOUGHTON MIFFLIN HARCOURT

10801 N. Mopac Expressway
Building # 3
Austin, TX 78759
1.800.531.5015

Steck-Vaughn is a trademark of HMH Supplemental Publishers Inc. registered in the United States of America and/or other jurisdictions. All inquiries should be mailed to HMH Supplemental Publishers Inc., P.O. Box 27010, Austin, TX 78755.

Rubicon
www.rubiconpublishing.com

Project Editors: Miriam Bardswich, Kim Koh
Editorial Assistants: Kermin Bhot, Andrea Jenkins
Art/Creative Director: Jennifer Drew
Assistant Art Director: Jen Harvey
Designer: Jeanette Debusschere
Cover image–Cover image–Nasa; [Igor Chekalin; Juha Sompinmäki; djgis; Galyna Andrushko] Shutterstock.com; title page–Jason and Bonnie Grower/ Shutterstock.com

Printed in Singapore

ISBN: 978-1-4190-2400-9
3 4 5 6 7 8 9 10 11 12 2016 22 21 20 19 18 17 16 15 14 13 12 13
A B C D E F G

CONTENTS

4 Introduction: Our Place in the Universe

6 Solar System
An interplanetary article about our solar system.

8 Journey
The spirit of adventure is alive and well in this poem about exploring the galaxies.

9 A Weighty Subject!
Ever wonder what keeps the planets circling the sun? It's the same stuff that keeps your feet on the ground. An informational article about gravity.

12 How Fast Is Fast?
What's the fastest thing in the universe? Turn quickly to this article and find out!

14 Baseball on the Asteroid
Yup. Just what it says. Read these instructions to learn how to play asteroid baseball.

16 Space Travel
3 … 2 …1 … 0 … Liftoff! Check out the exploits of real-life space exploration in this timeline.

21 Journey to Mars
Check out this ad and brochure for a vacation on Mars that might happen in the not-so-distant future.

24 Hello Earth
Your mom just sent you an email — from outer space!

26 A One-way Trip
Next time you're in space, try to avoid the black holes. This informational article explains why.

30 World of the Small
Check out this teeny-weeny explanation of the incredible world of nanotechnology.

32 Outer Space
Space — the final frontier. An article about interplanetary travel and extraterrestrial intelligence.

34 Search for the Lost Code
Can scientists prevent the total destruction of a planet? Find out in this gripping graphic story with a twist.

38 Into the Future
How do you shorten time spent on space travel? You build a space drive — naturally! Here are descriptions of a few ideas.

41 Lone Wolf Sees the Sky
Would you like to see into the future? Read this fictional story to find out how Leon Wolf did it.

46 Millennium Dance
A poem about dreams of the future and memories of the past.

Our Place in the Universe

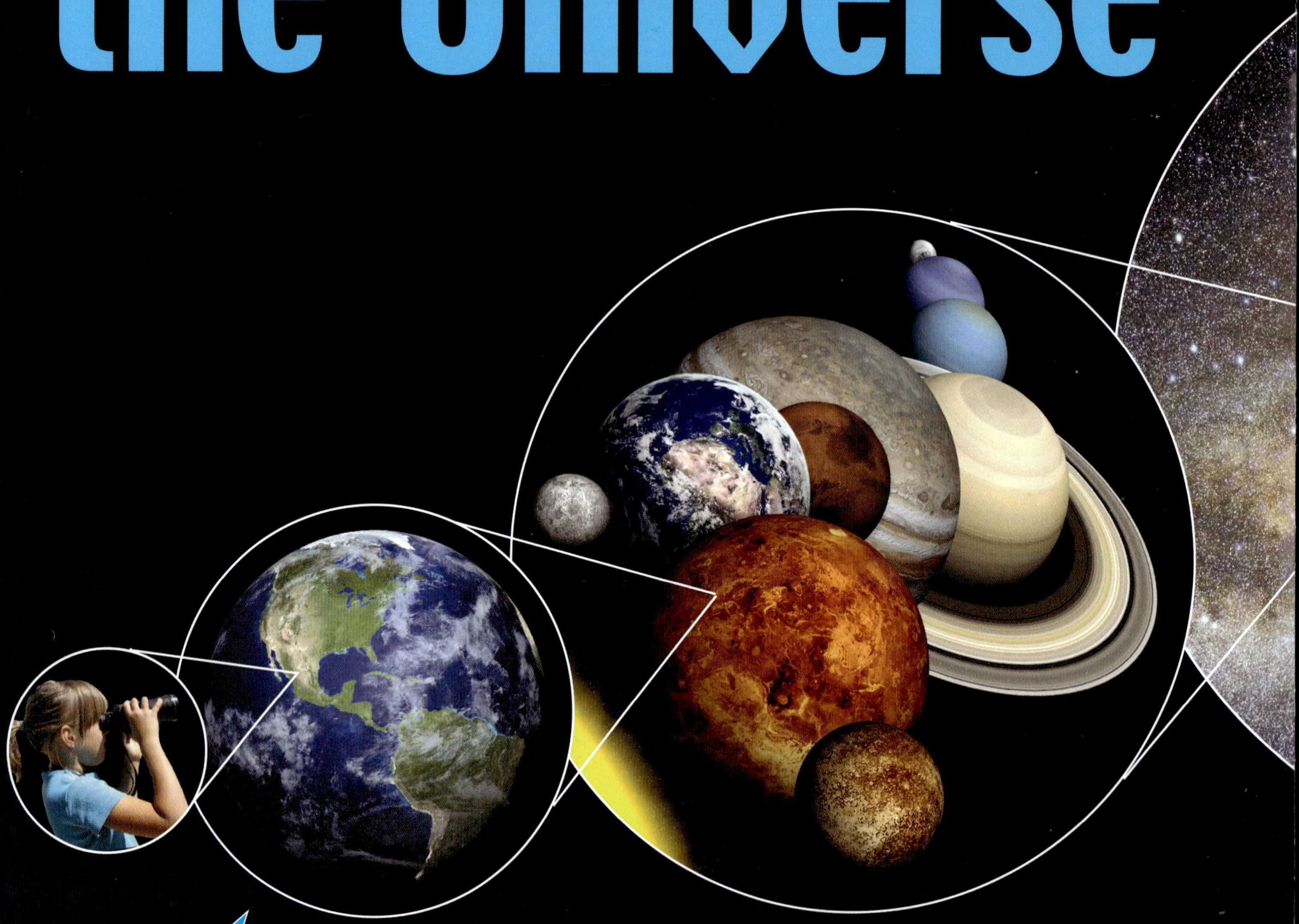

EARTH
Earth is a small planet in the solar system and only a tiny speck of rock in the whole universe.

SOLAR SYSTEM
The solar system is made up of nine planets, a star, and other smaller bodies. It is only a part of the Milky Way Galaxy.

THE UNIVERSE

The universe is huge — it is bigger than we can ever imagine. Everything that exists — including space and time — is contained in the universe.

GALAXY

A galaxy is an incredibly large collection of stars, gas, and dust. Our Milky Way Galaxy is only one of billions of galaxies in the whole universe.

Girl, Earth–iStockphoto; [planets–oorka; Milky Way–Viktar Malyshchyts] Shutterstock.com

Solar System

warm up

What picture immediately comes to mind when you see the title? Is it like what you see on these pages? How is it similar or different?

The solar system is about six billion years old. It is made up of a star, nine planets, and many moons, asteroids, and comets. Each planet orbits (goes around) the sun — the only star in the solar system. It takes Earth 365.25 days to orbit the sun.

ASTEROIDS

Asteroids are rocky objects that orbit the sun. They are too small to be called "planets." An asteroid belt is located between Mars and Jupiter.

METEORS

Some asteroids can get close to the Earth and get caught by the Earth's gravity. These are called "meteors." When a meteor flies through the Earth's atmosphere, friction burns most of it away. If the remains of the meteor hit the Earth, it is called a "meteorite."

A hole left in the Earth after a meteorite hit

PLANETS

The nine planets, beginning with the closest to the sun, are Mercury, Venus, Earth, Mars, Jupiter, Saturn, Uranus, Neptune, and Pluto.

Mercury, Venus, and Mars are called terrestrial planets. This means they have a hard, rocky surface, like Earth.

Jupiter, Saturn, Uranus, and Neptune are gas planets. They have no hard surface and are made up mainly of gas.

The planet closest to the sun is Mercury (36 million miles). The planet furthest from the sun is Pluto (3,700 million miles).

wrap up

In a small group, brainstorm and list words to describe a planet, an asteroid, a meteor, and a comet. Write a caption for each of them, using any three words from your list.

COMETS

Comets are lumps of ice and dust. Comets release vast clouds of gas and dust as they travel. The most famous comet is Halley's Comet, which orbits the sun once every 76 years.

WEB CONNECTIONS

For a look at the solar system, visit **http://solarsystem.nasa.gov/index.cfm** on the Internet. Check out any one planet, and put together some information about this planet to share with your friends.

JOURNEY

THE TIME TO GO IS NOW!
OUR JOURNEY BEGINS AT DAWN ...
THE GALAXIES AWAIT.

PIONEERS WITH HOPES AND DREAMS
JOIN THE QUEST OF DISCOVERY ...
THE GALAXIES AWAIT.

CONTACT HAS BEEN MADE!
THEY KNOW WE ARE READY ...
THE GALAXIES AWAIT.

THE NEW TIME IS HERE!
WE'LL SHINE AMONG THE STARS ...
FOR THE GALAXIES AWAIT!

By Robert Cutting

wrap up

1. Imagine you are one of the pioneers in this poem. Make a list of things that you hope to discover in the galaxies.

2. Have you ever wanted to go somewhere really different? Write a description or make a sketch of a place, real or imaginary, that you would like to visit.

WEB CONNECTIONS

Visit this website to see some incredible pictures of galaxies: **www.maa.mhn.de/Scholar/galaxy_pic.html**. What did you find most interesting? Share it with your class.

warm up

Gravity is the force that makes things fall to the ground on Earth. Think of three everyday things that would change if there was no gravity.

A Weighty Subject!

You jump into the air, and very quickly you come back down to the ground. Why don't you just keep going higher until you reach outer space? Simple — it's gravity that stops you from going any higher.

So, what is gravity? Gravity is a force of attraction between things that have mass. The bigger the mass of something, the greater its gravity.

The Earth has a lot more mass than you do. When you jump, the Earth's gravity pulls you back to the ground.

FYI

Objects on Earth have a point, called their center of gravity. A lower center of gravity makes an object more stable. Cars are designed with engines near the ground to keep their center of gravity low. This way, they can go around a corner quickly without tipping over.

Gravity is what keeps the planets orbiting around the sun. The sun is so much larger than any of the planets, and it has much more mass than all of the planets combined. So it has a greater gravitational pull, and it keeps all of the planets going around it. If the sun were not there, the Earth and the other planets would go off in different directions into deep space.

◂ Gravity also keeps the moon orbiting around the Earth. Can you guess why? The Earth has more mass than the moon, so it has a greater gravitational pull. It keeps the moon going around it.

As you can see, gravity is a very important force on the Earth and in the universe. Can we see gravity? No, but we can show what it does. Albert Einstein, a famous scientist, once said that mass "bends" or "curves" space. The greater the mass of an object (like a planet or a star), the greater is the bend in space. You can show this by doing the following experiment. You need these items: a bedsheet, three kinds of balls (sponge ball, volleyball, and basketball), and a heavy object (large rock).

◂ This astronaut floats weightlessly in outer space where there is zero gravity.

Astronaut–Nasa; all other images–Shutterstock

EXPERIMENT

1. Get six friends to hold the bedsheet, three on each side. Have them stretch it out so that it is flat, at chest height.

2. Take the sponge ball and roll it onto the stretched-out bedsheet. Do the same with the volleyball and the basketball. Notice that the bedsheet curves down each time you place a ball on it.

3. Take the rock and place it near the center of the stretched-out bedsheet. Did the bedsheet curve farther down?

4. Now, leaving the rock where it is, take the sponge ball and roll it onto the stretched-out bedsheet. You may want to try this with the other balls as well. Did all the balls roll toward the rock on the bedsheet?

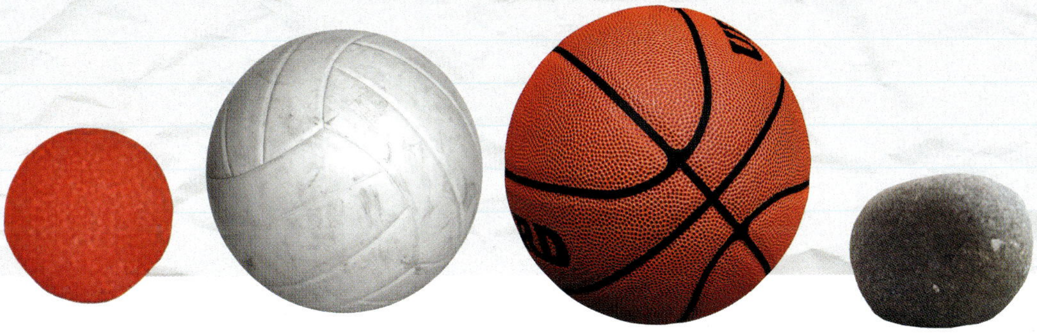

Imagine the stretched-out bedsheet as outer space. When there is no mass in space, there is no bend or curve. When you put an object with a little mass (sponge ball) into "space," it bends or curves space slightly. When you put a very massive object (like a rock) into "space," it bends or curves space a great deal. And, when another object with less mass than the rock is placed onto "space," it moves toward the more massive object (the rock).

This is how gravity can be shown! Think about gravity the next time you jump. It's really gravity that is pulling you back to the ground. Without gravity, all of us would be flying off into space!

wrap up

1. In your own words, explain what gravity does.
2. In small groups, try out this experiment and note what happens. Describe the result in a short paragraph.

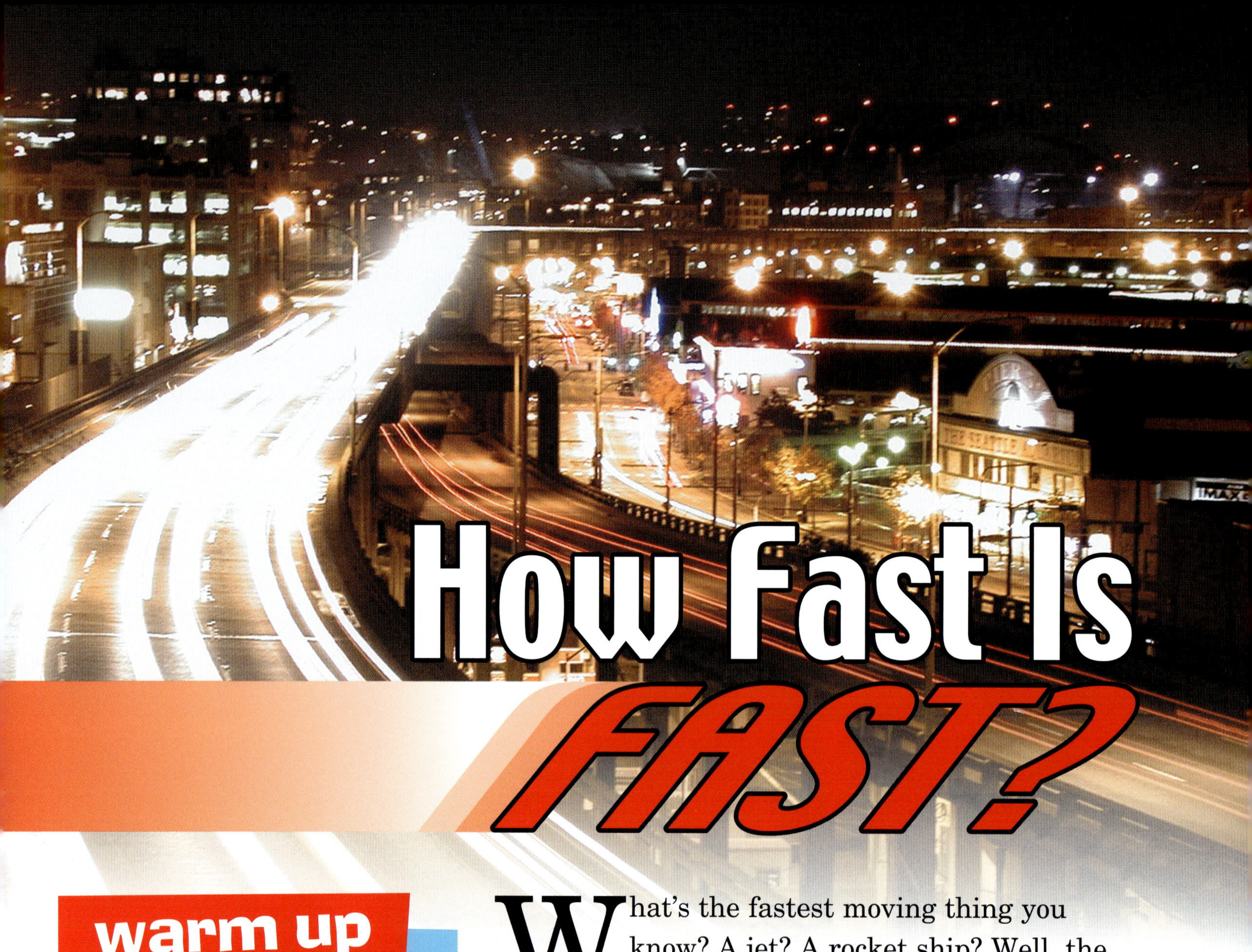

How Fast Is FAST?

warm up

Besides vehicles, what else in your daily life requires speed? Is speed always a good thing?

What's the fastest moving thing you know? A jet? A rocket ship? Well, the fastest moving thing in the universe is light! That's right! Nothing that we know of can go faster than light. So, how fast does light travel?

Light travels 186,000 miles in one second! If you had a very powerful light and someone stood 186,000 miles away, he or she would see your light one second after you turned on the switch. If you were 372,000 miles away, he or she would see the light two seconds after you turned on the switch, and so on.

CHECKPOINT

Do the math. How far would you be from the light if it took 10 seconds to reach you?

When scientists talk about how far things are in the solar system, they often use the terms light-seconds, light-minutes, or light-hours. In space travel, we talk about light-years.

City lights–iStockphoto; [sunbather–Vasaleks, sun–Lasse Kristensen] Shutterstock.com

What is a light-year? A light-year is a measure of distance, not time. It is the distance that light will travel in one year at the speed of light. It means simply that in one year, light will have traveled a certain distance, moving at 186,000 miles/sec.

How far is that distance? Get ready! This is a very big number — about 5,900,000,000,000 miles! That's 5 trillion, 900 billion miles! So, a light-year is a very long distance.

How far are the stars and galaxies in the universe from the Earth? The closest star system to us is the Alpha Centauri system, approximately 4.3 light-years away. So, to find out how far that is, multiply 4.3 by 5,900,000,000,000 miles and you get … well, a really BIG number! And remember, Alpha Centauri is the closest star system to us. All the rest are farther away than that!

Could we ever travel as fast as light? Who knows? Maybe someday we will discover a way of traveling that fast. Until then, we will have to be content with trips to the moon.

CHECKPOINT

Looking at the big numbers, think of three words to describe the size of the universe.

wrap up

In a chart, list the five fastest things you know of and write a short description of each. Compare your chart with a friend's. What's the same? What's different?

WEB CONNECTIONS

Use the Internet to check out the speed of light. Which planet is closest to the sun? Which is the farthest from the sun?

Baseball on the Asteroid

warm up

Have you ever played baseball or watched a baseball game? Can you imagine playing baseball on a planet in space? What would it be like?

You have decided to take a vacation in space, and you have just landed on an asteroid called Ida that orbits between Mars and Jupiter. There is not much gravity here, so you have to be careful not to jump too high.

So, what do you do on this tiny asteroid, when you want to have some fun? You play baseball, of course! And all by yourself.

Here's what you do: Open up your space pack and take out your baseball, your bat, and your glove.

Now, hold the baseball bat like you are going to hit a ball into the outfield. (No, there's no outfield on the asteroid, just rock!) Lift up the baseball. Slowly and gently, toss the ball up in front of you. It will go up for a while, and then the gravity of Ida will capture it and slowly bring it back down to you. As the baseball gets closer to you, get ready to bat it away.

Here it comes, wait for it ... wait for it ... There!

Now you can bat it! But, bat it very carefully and without much force!

Illustrations by Jeremy Bennison

You don't want to send the baseball off into space! Okay, you've hit the ball with just a little force. Watch it, there it goes! It's flying off toward the horizon. Now, you can see it slipping below the horizon. That's because you've hit the ball with just enough force to send it into orbit around Ida!

Now, you've got to wait.

Maybe you want to take out a book from your space pack and read. Or catch up on that video game you've been playing. Whatever you decide to do, you have about 30 minutes. So, sit on a rock and just relax!

Now, it's been 30 minutes. Time to get up and put the book or video game down. Pick up the baseball glove and put it on. Turn around and face the opposite direction. Get ready, wait for it ... wait for it ... There! The ball is coming over the other horizon toward you. It's getting closer ... stick your glove hand up and ... You caught it! Great job!

So, that's how you play baseball on the asteroid. You don't even need a team!

The next time you vacation on Ida, you might want to try hockey.

wrap up

1. What is the difference between playing baseball on Earth and on Ida? What causes this difference?
2. With a partner, decide on another sport, such as hockey or tennis, which you would like to play on the asteroid. What are some things to consider? Write the instructions for playing the game.

WEB CONNECTIONS

To find out more about asteroids, visit **www.enchantedlearning.com/subjects/astronomy/asteroids/**. Then try out the quiz on this site.

SPACE TRAVEL

Since the 1960s, many space explorers have gone into space. These astronauts have traveled in rockets and space shuttles. They have walked on the moon, and they have stayed in space for long periods of time in space stations. Read about their explorations in this timeline.

warm up

What comes to mind when you read the title? Would you jump at the chance to travel in space?

1961

Yuri A. Gagarin from the Soviet Union was the first man in space. He orbited the Earth once.

1962

John Glenn Jr. became the first American astronaut to orbit the Earth three times.

1963

Soviet cosmonaut Valentina Tereshkova became the first woman in space and orbited the Earth 48 times.

1965

- A Soviet cosmonaut made the first space walk for 12 minutes.
- An American astronaut made the first space walk for 22 minutes.
- The spacecraft *Mariner 4* transmitted the first pictures of Mars.

1967

- Three American astronauts were killed in a fire on the launch pad.
- A Soviet cosmonaut was killed in a crash when his parachute failed to open.

All images—NASA

1969

Apollo 11 landed on the moon. Neil Armstrong and Edwin Aldrin Jr. became the first men from Earth to walk on the moon.

1970

- Soviet automatic spacecraft collected the first lunar soil samples.
- The first automatic robot landed on the moon.
- Soviet *Venera 7* landed on Venus.

1971

- The Soviets launched the space station *Salyut 1*, which remained in orbit until 1973.
- *Apollo 15* astronauts drove the first moon rover.

1972

US launched *Pioneer 10* towards Jupiter.

1973

US launched its first space station, the *Skylab*.

1975

US *Apollo 18* linked up with the Soviet *Soyuz* spacecraft and conducted joint experiments.

1976

Viking 2 landed on the Plain of Utopia in Mars, where it discovered water frost.

1979

- *Voyagers 1 & 2* began transmitting images of Jupiter and her moons.
- US probe reached Saturn and began transmitting images.

1981

US launched the first reusable space shuttle *Columbia*.

1984

- Svetlana Savitskaya became the first woman to walk in space.
- Katherine Sullivan was the first American woman to walk in space.

1986

- Russia launched the core unit of space station *Mir*.
- *Voyager 2* began transmitting images from Uranus.
- The space shuttle *Challenger* exploded after liftoff.

1989

Voyager 2 began transmitting images from Neptune.

1990

- The *Magellan* spacecraft began mapping the surface of Venus.
- The *Hubble Telescope* was set up in orbit. It was able to see deeper into space than any other telescope.

1991

Shuttle *Columbia* investigated the effects of weightlessness on human beings.

1995

- Russian cosmonaut Valeriy Polyakov set a new space endurance record. He stayed on *Mir* for 438 days.
- The *Galileo* probe began transmitting data from Jupiter.

1996

Thomas Reiter became the first European Space Agency astronaut to make two spacewalks.

1997

Mars Pathfinder became the first probe to land on Mars since 1976.

1998

John Glenn became the oldest man to fly in space at the age of 77.

1999

- Eileen Collins became the first female Shuttle Commander.
- China launched *Shenzhou*, its first unmanned test flight.

2001

- A spacecraft landed on the surface of the asteroid Eros.
- The Chinese launched a second test flight.
- The *Mir* space station broke up in the atmosphere and sank in the Pacific Ocean. It had been in space for 15 years.
- Business executive Dennis Tito paid $20 million to ride on the Russian *Soyuz* spacecraft. He became the first space tourist.

All images–NASA

2002

Mars probe, the *Odyssey*, found evidence of water beneath the surface of the planet.

2003

The space shuttle *Columbia* exploded on re-entry into the Earth's atmosphere. The crew on board were killed.

2004

- Two robotic explorers, *Spirit* and *Opportunity* were sent to Mars. *Spirit* landed on January 3rd and *Opportunity* on January 24th. They have been sending back pictures of Mars that have never been seen before.
- On June 21st, *SpaceShipOne* became the first private craft to leave the Earth's atmosphere and enter space.

SPACE ROCKET

There would be no space exploration without rockets. Unlike ordinary engines, a rocket carries its own supply of oxygen to burn its fuel.

Fuel is burned with oxygen in a combustion chamber to produce hot gases. The gases expand and stream backward out of the rocket, creating a force in the opposite direction. This force is called thrust, and it propels the rocket forward.

HOW THE SPACE SHUTTLE WORKS

The shuttle is made up of different units: the twin booster rockets, an orbiter that carries the crew, and an external fuel tank. Many parts of the shuttle can be used again, which is a big savings for the space program.

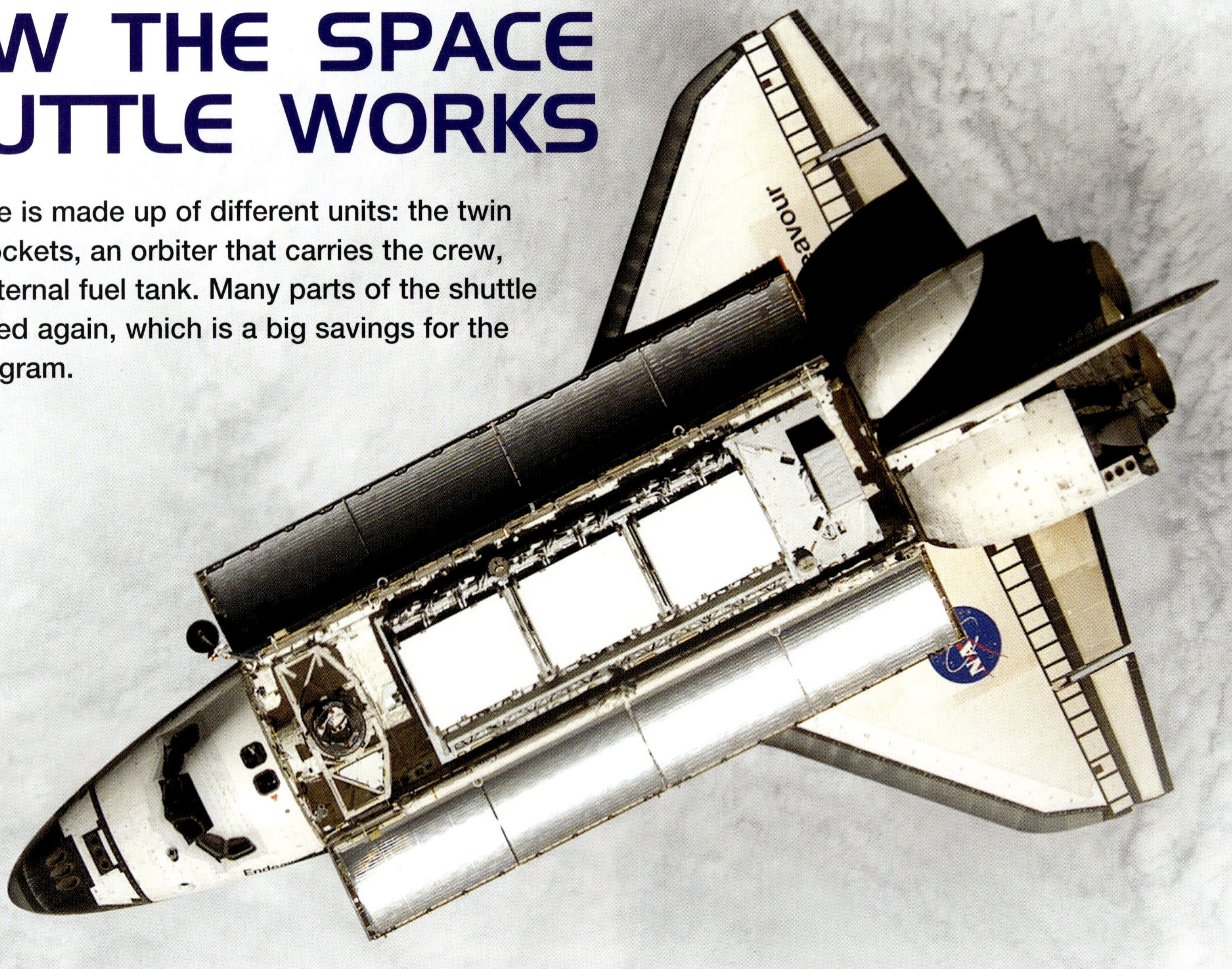

1. Orbiter engines and the rocket boosters all fire together during liftoff.
2. After liftoff, the rocket boosters separate and fall to Earth to be recovered from the sea.
3. A few minutes later, the fuel tank is dropped off; it burns off in the atmosphere.
4. Orbiter re-enters the atmosphere to return to Earth.
5. In the Earth's atmosphere, the orbiter flies like a glider; it lands on an airport runway.

wrap up

1. Using the information in this timeline, write a summary of the achievements in space exploration.
2. In a small group, create a collage about space exploration. You could include pictures of astronauts, cosmonauts, space rockets, space satellites, space shuttles, space stations, and probes. Write a caption for each picture.

WEB CONNECTIONS

Choose one astronaut or cosmonaut from the timeline. Gather more information about the person from the Internet or the library. Write a short profile to share with the class.

Space shuttle—NASA

JOURNEY TO MARS

Tired of the same old vacations?
Looking for new adventures?
Want the challenge of faraway planets?

Get away NOW! Check out our **SPECIAL OFFER**

INTERPLANETARY VACATIONS!

Stay in galactic comfort and enjoy stellar adventures

- The mountain splendors of Olympus Mons!
- The mighty canyons of Valles Marineris!
- The famous Martian "face" of Cydonia Mensae!

- 6,500 Monetary Credits for Luxury Class
- 8,500 Monetary Credits for Ultimate Class
- 12,500 Monetary Credits for Cosmic Class

Travel aboard the renowned space liner SS Galactia

Depart from Galactic Getaway's Interplanetary Spaceport

A choice of our famous hotels

- The Marble Inn of Olympus Mons
- The Canyon Lodge of Valles Marineris
- The Hill Cabins of Cydonia Mensae

Log on our Galactic Getaway website and click INTERPLANETARY VACATIONS

Mars and background–iStockphoto

warm up

Think of a "dream" vacation you would like to take with your friends. Share it with a partner.

WHAT CAN GALACTIC GETAWAY OFFER YOU?

Only the BEST in Interplanetary Vacations!
Three Martian Resorts!
Three Incredible Vacations!

OLYMPUS MONS: THE MARBLE INN

▲ Set at the base of Olympus Mons, the largest volcano in the solar system! A mountain lover's dream comes true!

▶ Practice on the amazing Rock Climbing Wall in the Marble Inn Gymnasium!

▲ Explore the deepest mountain crevices ever discovered! Climb the tallest peak in the solar system with your very own Climber Bot!

▲ Each Olympus Mons trip comes complete with a four-room suite, Butler Bot, and meals!

Robots, Geological formations–iStockphoto; Rock climber–greenland/Shutterstock.com

VALLES MARINERIS: THE CANYON LODGE

- Set at the edge of the mighty Valles Marineris canyon system in Candor Chasmata, near the Martian Equator! A canyon lover's dream comes true!

Walk for days along the manicured paths that weave throughout Valles Marineris! Study the rock formations in these ancient canyons!

- View the Valles Marineris canyon system as you fly through the canyon in your very own Fly Bot!

Each Valles Marineris trip comes complete with a two-building hut, Butler Bot, and meals.

CYDONIA MENSAE: THE HILL CABINS

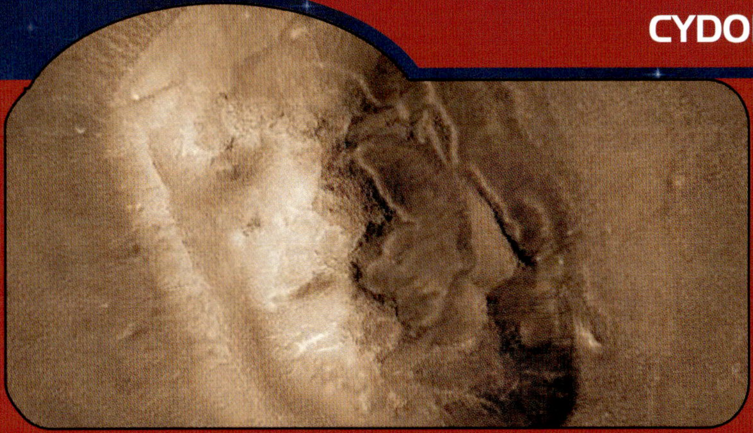

- Set at the base of Cydonia Mensae, the famous Martian "face"! An explorer's dream comes true!

Each Cydonia Mensae trip comes complete with a three-room hill cabin, Butler Bot, and all meals.

- Tour the many geological formations that are to be found at Cydonia Mensae!

Don't delay! Book your vacation today! Log on our Galactic Getaway website and contact the Operator Bot on your holoscreen.

wrap up

1. Study the ad and the brochure. With a friend, discuss which resort you think would be the best one to visit. Give reasons for your choice.
2. Email Interplanetary Vacations to make your reservations. Be as detailed as you can.

HELLO EARTH

From:	Major Michelle Laura Matthews
To:	Derek Matthews
Subject:	We Made It!

warm up

Imagine you're on a journey to Mars. Visualize what you would see.

CHECKPOINT

Pick out clues that show this journey was not made in the 20th century.

I can't believe I'm talking to you from outer space! Just yesterday, we were waiting for liftoff on the launch pad. I remember feeling so glad that I wasn't in an old rocket as I sat in the cockpit of *Solar One*, waiting for the countdown to begin. Soon it was "... 5, 4, 3, 2, 1, 0 ... and we are on our way to Mars!"

In a few seconds, we were above Earth. The view was incredible! We were very comfortable in our navigation seats, watching the Earth get smaller as we climbed into the sky. You don't see countries, Derek, just one planet. It's so beautiful!

Once in space, we navigated the ship to the moon base. After a short stop to pick up supplies, we were ready for the journey to Mars. Taking off from the moon, by the way, was much easier! It has only one-sixth the Earth's gravity,

---

liftoff: *the vertical takeoff of a spacecraft or rocket*
navigation: *managing the course of a ship*

Earth–Denis Tabler/Shutterstock.com

so we got off the surface with just a little thrust from the engines. We raced into interplanetary space. We got the ship up to full power, reaching speeds only dreamed of in the old days of space exploration.

Then we set the artificial gravity in the ship so we could move about as we do on Earth. I have never liked weightlessness. It's too difficult to get anything done properly when you are floating around! Mind you, it was fun when we turned off the artificial gravity to play a game of anti-gravity volleyball. We had a very interesting match, with the ball going everywhere in the large meeting room. It was quite something to watch! Astronauts floating up, pushing off the ship walls, bouncing into each other! We laughed more than we played!

Oops, now it's time for me to check the ship's guidance systems. It will be another 12 days before we reach Mars. Say "Hi!" to everyone at home for me.

You have a great day!

Love, Mom

---

thrust: *a push with sudden force*
interplanetary: *relating to travel between planets*

FYI

Two robots are now exploring Mars. They are sending back amazing images and new information about the planet. Will people be sent to Mars soon? The concerns are gravity and the time it would take to get there. A mission to Mars would last at least two and a half years. Now that's a long time to be without gravity!

CHECKPOINT

Why would it not be possible to play volleyball the way we play the game on the Earth?

wrap up

Imagine you are Derek, and you've just received this email from your mom. Reply to her email. Describe how you felt and what you saw from the ground.

WEB CONNECTIONS

With a partner or two, gather more information about Mars on the Internet. Create a poster to announce the next Mars mission and to attract astronauts for a trip to this planet.

A ONE-WAY TRIP

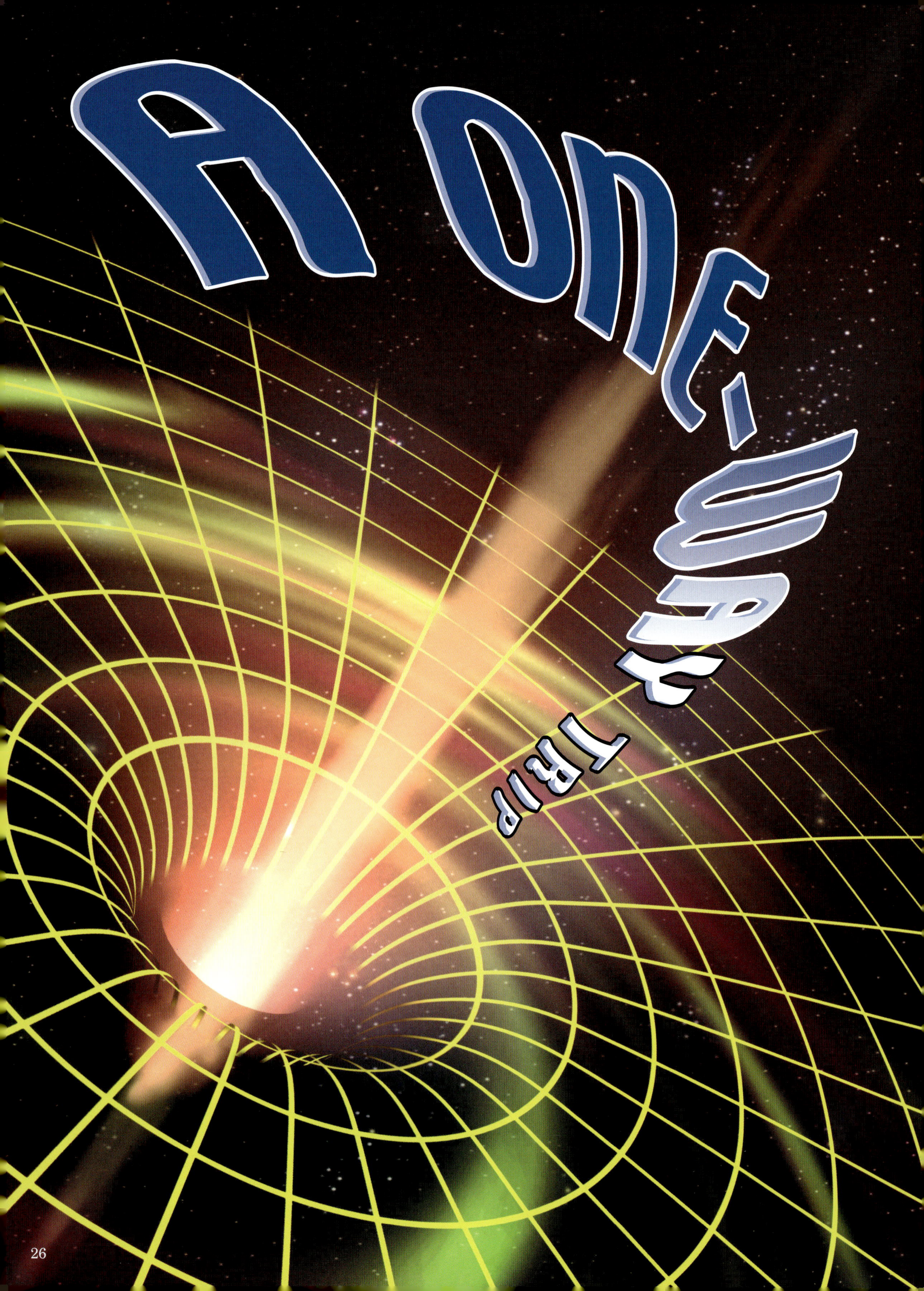

warm up

Have you ever had a nightmare about falling? In a small group, share different "falling" stories.

If you plan on a trip into space, you might get more than you bargained for! You might fly into a black hole and never return!

What is a black hole?

A black hole is really not a hole at all. It is the remains of a massive star that has caved in on itself. This happens when a star has used up all of its fuel. When the fuel is all gone, the star's gravity becomes so intense that it pulls the star inward. The star collapses into a single point, and the space around this point is a black hole. Anything that gets too close to the black hole will be pulled in by the intense gravity. Nothing that falls in can escape from it, not even light!

FYI

Stars burn gas as their fuel. They change hydrogen gas into helium gas. When this happens, stars give off light.

How big are black holes?

Black holes can be very small, about a few miles across. They can be very large, millions of miles across.

FYI

There is a very large black hole at the center of our Milky Way Galaxy. Scientists think that most galaxies have black holes at their centers.

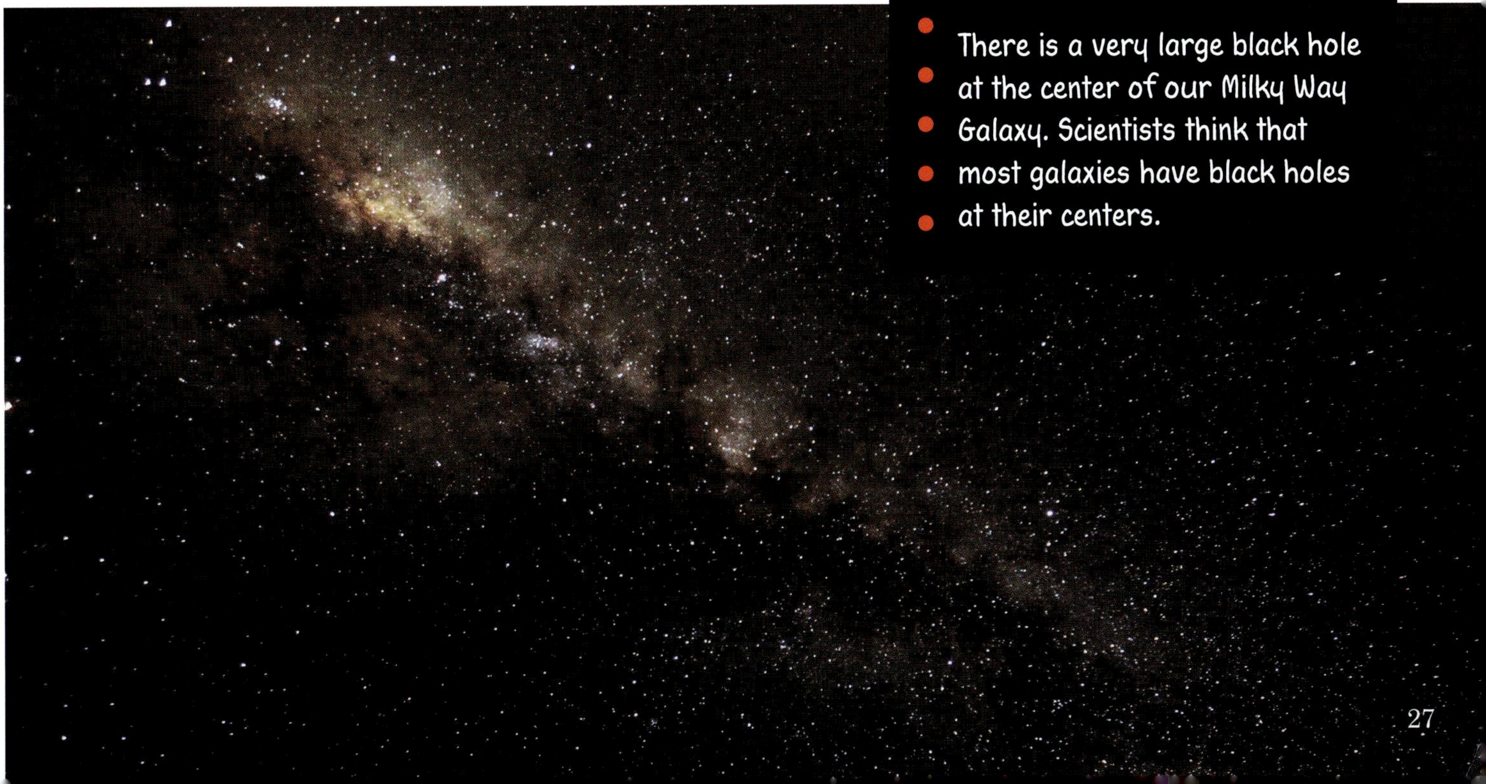

[Black hole– Andrea Danti; Milky Way–MACHKAZU, Yellow star–HomeArt] Shutterstockcom

☆ Will our sun ever become a black hole?

No. Thankfully, the sun is too small to become a black hole. Black holes are formed from stars that are at least two to three times the size of the sun.

FYI

Our sun has at least another five billion years to go before it runs out of fuel. When it does, it will get bigger and become a giant red star.

☆ Can we see black holes?

No, since light can't escape from them, we can't see them. However, we can guess that there is a black hole when we get X-rays or energy coming from a dark place in space.

☆ What happens if you get too close to a black hole?

The edge of a black hole is called the "event horizon." If you were watching a person close to the event horizon, you would notice some

[Boy–Tischenko Irina; sun–James Thew] Shutterstock.com

waves reflecting from the person's body. As the light waves get longer, they become red in color.

The person near the black hole would also feel something very strange. The gravity would stretch the person out like spaghetti! And the gravity would pull so hard that the person would be drawn in fast, like water down a cosmic drain. Soon, the person would spiral into the black hole, with no way of ever getting out again.

What is a one-way trip?

So, get too close to a black hole and you get a one-way trip into space. Oh, yes, into space. What is meant by that? Well, scientists think that black holes do something interesting to space itself. They think that black holes create pathways into other universes! Will we ever find out if this is true? Probably not. Remember: it's a one-way trip into a black hole!

Fall in, and you'll never be able to come back and tell what you found!

wrap up

1. In a short paragraph, describe what changes occur if someone gets too close to a black hole.
2. Is this a one-way trip that you would like to make? Explain why or why not.

WEB CONNECTIONS

Watch a movie on "approaching the black hole" on the Internet. You could use this website: **http://casa.colorado.edu/~ajsh/orbit.html**.

WORLD

warm up

Imagine you are an insect. Discuss with a friend what everyday life would be like for you.

CHECKPOINT

Say "na-no-tek-nall-oh-gee" aloud. Did you trip over the word?

Some things are small, like insects or grains of sand. Some things are really small, like germs or cells. Some things are so small, you cannot see them even with a microscope. Then think of an atom — the smallest particle of a substance.

Welcome to the world of nanotechnology! Nanotechnology is the ability to make incredibly small things, at the nanometer size. A nanometer is one-billionth of a meter. That means you could fit one billion things that are only a nanometer on a meter stick. Now, that's small!

An artist's impression of nanobots and red blood cells

OF THE SMALL

Scientists believe that in the near future, they will be able to create tiny machines that will be no bigger than a nanometer in size. These machines would be much stronger and better. For example, we could have a super computer the size of a cell phone.

Nanotechnology will change space exploration. Spaceships that have parts built using nanotechnology would be very strong. They would be able to withstand the harshness of space during long space flights.

Another use for nanotechnology is in the medical field. Many scientists think that one day we will be able to cure diseases by injecting millions of nanobots, tiny robots that are at the nanometer size, into a person. The nanobots would go to the diseased spot in the body and remove the disease. The person would then be cured.

Today, many laboratories are working on making nanotechnology a reality. Scientists believe that we will see nanobots and other tiny machines very soon.

FYI

In 2004, scientists at New York University created a 10-nanometer-long microscopic walking robot, the smallest of its kind.

wrap up

1. In your own words, explain how nanotechnology can help a person with a disease.
2. Imagine you and a partner are scientists. Create a poster to tell people what you know about nanotechnology.

WEB CONNECTIONS

Go to **www.sciencenewsforkids.org.** With a partner, read any one article on the site. Write a summary.

Outer Space

warm up

Think of a story you have read or a movie you have seen that involves outer space. Did you enjoy it? Why or why not?

It has always been a human desire to go into outer space and explore the planets. But is this possible? Do we have the speed to do manned interplanetary travel?

Scientists around the world are working to discover new ways of moving faster in space. One day, they may find the answers. For now, we will have to be content with space flights to planets closer to the Earth.

CHECKPOINT

Here's something to think about.

Do we send people or robots into outer space to discover unknown planets? Many scientists believe only robots should explore space because an accident involving a robot causes the loss of a machine and not a life. Other scientists argue that only people can make observations that are needed to advance human life. What do you think?

interplanetary: *between planets*

FYI

Scientists launched interplanetary missions to study planets, asteroids, and comets. The first successful interplanetary craft flew past Venus in 1962.

Exploring Mars

Some of the most exciting interplanetary missions have been to Mars. It is the only other planet where life forms may once have existed and where human beings could possibly settle in the future. In January 2004, two robot vehicles touched down on Mars. They are now exploring the planet — gathering soil samples and sending pictures of the planet.

Alien Life Forms

What about exploration by other life forms? Will we ever be "discovered" by beings from other planets? If we believe in the stories about alien visitors, then distant travelers might have visited and studied us for many years. Many people believe that aliens have been here, while others think aliens belong to science fiction.

The Search

A worldwide group, SETI (Search for Extraterrestrial Intelligence), is monitoring the skies for signals from intelligent life forms in outer space. It hopes to eventually discover proof that alien life exists. If SETI is correct, science fiction and science fact will become a blur. And we will go into a future that is beyond reality, beyond the imagination!

---

extraterrestrial: *from outer space*

WEB CONNECTIONS

Visit the website **www.nasa.gov** and click "Humans in Space" to get information about living and working in space.

wrap up

1. In a small group, discuss the main ideas presented in this article. Express your group's opinion for each idea. Be prepared to explain your view.
2. Imagine you work for SETI and you want to reach out to a life form in space. Write a short message to introduce yourself and to explain that you wish to be a friend.

Space background–Jurgen Ziewe; Blue background–ssuaphotos/Shutterstock.com; Alien, Satellites–iStockphoto; Mars exploration–NASA

SEARCH FOR THE LOST CODE

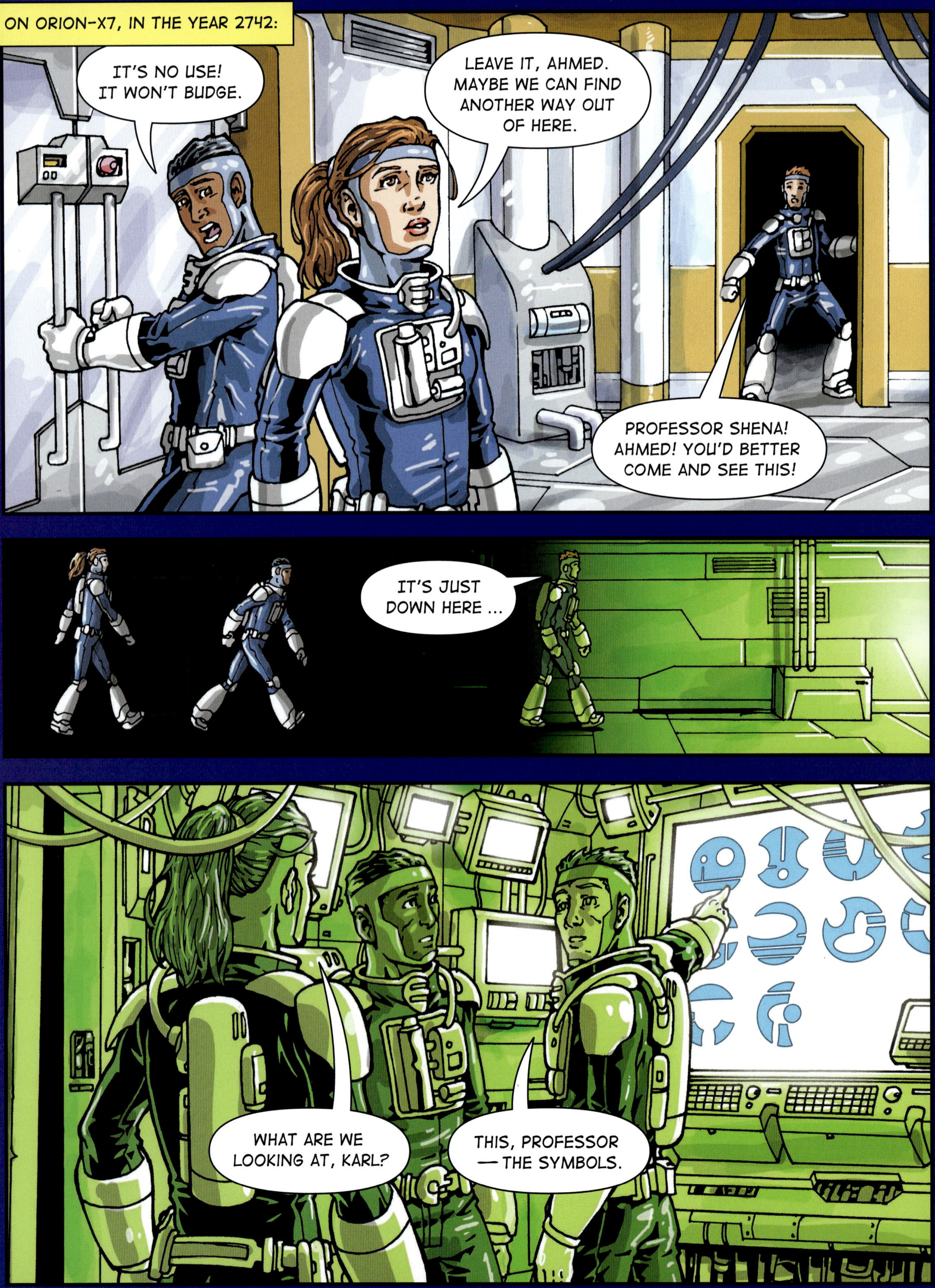

ON ORION-X7, IN THE YEAR 2742:
IT'S NO USE! IT WON'T BUDGE.
LEAVE IT, AHMED. MAYBE WE CAN FIND ANOTHER WAY OUT OF HERE.
PROFESSOR SHENA! AHMED! YOU'D BETTER COME AND SEE THIS!
IT'S JUST DOWN HERE ...
WHAT ARE WE LOOKING AT, KARL?
THIS, PROFESSOR — THE SYMBOLS.

Illustrated by JEREMY BENNISON

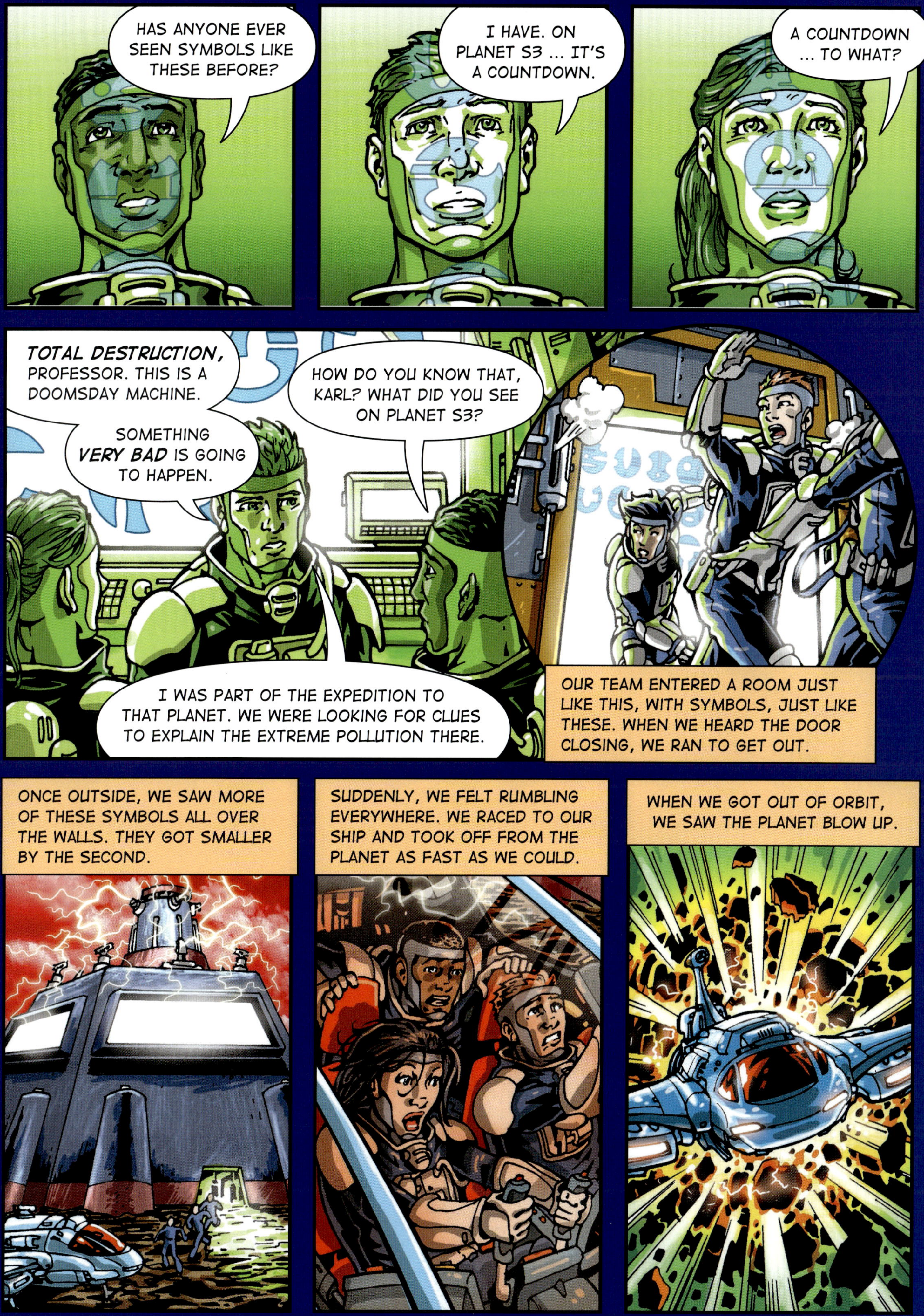
HAS ANYONE EVER SEEN SYMBOLS LIKE THESE BEFORE?
I HAVE. ON PLANET S3 ... IT'S A COUNTDOWN.
A COUNTDOWN ... TO WHAT?
TOTAL DESTRUCTION, PROFESSOR. THIS IS A DOOMSDAY MACHINE.
SOMETHING VERY BAD IS GOING TO HAPPEN.
HOW DO YOU KNOW THAT, KARL? WHAT DID YOU SEE ON PLANET S3?
I WAS PART OF THE EXPEDITION TO THAT PLANET. WE WERE LOOKING FOR CLUES TO EXPLAIN THE EXTREME POLLUTION THERE.
OUR TEAM ENTERED A ROOM JUST LIKE THIS, WITH SYMBOLS, JUST LIKE THESE. WHEN WE HEARD THE DOOR CLOSING, WE RAN TO GET OUT.
ONCE OUTSIDE, WE SAW MORE OF THESE SYMBOLS ALL OVER THE WALLS. THEY GOT SMALLER BY THE SECOND.
SUDDENLY, WE FELT RUMBLING EVERYWHERE. WE RACED TO OUR SHIP AND TOOK OFF FROM THE PLANET AS FAST AS WE COULD.
WHEN WE GOT OUT OF ORBIT, WE SAW THE PLANET BLOW UP.

WE FIGURED THE SPECIES HAD CREATED A DOOMSDAY MACHINE TO DESTROY THE PLANET.
THEIR PLANET HAD BEEN DESTROYED BY POLLUTION. THEY HAD RUN OUT OF FUEL, FOOD AND WATER. THE PLANET BECAME LIFELESS, SO THEY DESTROYED IT.
WELL WE'D BETTER GET OUTTA HERE -- BUT THE DOOR IS LOCKED!
I THINK THERE MAY BE ANOTHER WAY, PROFESSOR! WE CAN STOP THE COUNTDOWN!
HOW?
AFTER WE GOT AWAY FROM PLANET S3, WE DOWN-LOADED ALL THE DATA THAT WE'D SCANNED. WE DISCOVERED THIS SET OF SYMBOLS.
ONE WAS MISSING.
IF WE CAN FIND IT, WE CAN TYPE IT INTO THE COMPUTER AND STOP THE COUNTDOWN.
IT'S TOO LATE! LOOK!

wrap up

1. Explain the ending of the story. Are you surprised it ended this way?
2. With a partner, discuss if you would like this video game. Why or why not?

INTO THE FUTURE

warm up

What is the longest trip you have taken? What did you like or not like about this trip? Talk to your friends about your experience.

In the last 40 years, a lot has changed in space travel. Yet today's space ships are still traveling at about the same speed they did in the 1960s.

The spaceships we have now would take years to reach the nearest planets. Why? The distance between Earth and the other planets and stars can be billions, even trillions of miles!

So, how do we get from Earth to the planets or other star systems without taking so long? Invent a space drive, of course!

[Space–Molodec; spaceship–DM7] Shutterstock.com

What is a Space Drive?

A space drive is a way of propelling a spaceship faster than anything we have now. In the television program *Star Trek*, the starship *USS Enterprise* used a space drive called a "warp drive," which allowed the ship to travel faster than the speed of light.

A warp drive does not exist now. To have something that could match it in speed, we need rocket engines that would allow spaceships to travel much faster than they can now.

Solar Sails

One way to propel a spaceship in space is to use light from stars, such as the sun. NASA is working on a way to make this happen by using solar sails. These sails would be made of a very thin material, and would be spread over about one-third of a mile in space. The sail would gather light from the sun and use it to increase its speed. As the light hits the sail, it would move the sail and the spaceship that is attached to it faster. The sail would act like a giant reflector in space. Using a solar sail, NASA hopes to get a spacecraft up to speeds that are at least five times faster than any spaceship today.

Starship–[PARAMOUNT TELEVISION / THE KOBAL COLLECTION]; solar sail–NASA

propelling: *driving or pushing forward*

solar: *having to do with the sun*

Bussard Engine

In 1960, a scientist by the name of Robert Bussard came up with the idea of making a new type of rocket engine. It is called the Bussard Ramjet. It works differently from the rocket engines we have today. What the Bussard Ramjet would do is collect hydrogen from space, compress it, and then use it as a fuel to power the engines. The rocket engine would not have to carry a fuel supply as it would collect its fuel during its trip in space itself. As it collects more fuel, it would be able to go faster and faster.

New space drives and rocket engines might be the way for us to get out into space and travel great distances. Much work still needs to be done. It is possible that one day, we will be traveling to the planets and the stars aboard spaceships with engines that work very differently from the rockets we have today.

compress: *to press together into a smaller space*

FYI

- Hydrogen is everywhere in space.
- It would be very easy for the Ramjet
- to collect this gas as it flew in space.

wrap up

Imagine what space travel would be like 100 years from now. In a small group, create a storyboard to tell the story. In different frames, show the dressing of the astronauts, the inside and outside of the spacecraft, the liftoff, the speed of travel, and the other planets in space. Through the dialogues, indicate the destination and the goal of the mission.

Bussard Ramjet–NASA

LONE WOLF SEES THE SKY

Who are the keepers of the family's stories? What stories do they tell? How do their stories influence their young? Meet a Mohawk family whose members have been space explorers over the years.

Sometime in the Present

Leon Wolf enjoyed his daily walks with his Grandfather. His parents had died when he was born, 12 years ago and his Grandfather had looked after him. On their walks, Leon's Grandfather would talk to him about his parents and the history of his people, the Kanien k' haka (Gan-yen-k-ha-ga) or Mohawk. Leon loved to listen to the stories and the many wise sayings from his Grandfather.

Today's walk had started the same way. They strolled through the woods and fields just down the hill from town. At night, they settled down on the same grassy patch, made a small fire, and looked at the star-filled sky. Leon's Grandfather reached into his travel bag and took out a silvery object.

"You've brought binoculars, Grandfather!" Leon said happily. "Now we will really be able to see the stars and planets close up!"

warm up

It is always a treat to listen to family stories. Think of your favorite family story and share it with a group of friends.

CHECKPOINT

Say the name of the Mohawk aloud. Did you pronounce it correctly without the guide?

FYI

The Mohawk people are a member of the Iroquois, now living in parts of northern New York and southern Ontario. In the past, their lands were in what is now upper New York State, Quebec along the St. Lawrence River, and eastern Ontario. The name of the Mohawk — Kanien k' haka — means "People of the Flint."

"You're right," said his Grandfather, "but not in the way you think." He handed the binoculars to Leon. The silver color glistened. Two dials shone in the firelight.

"Grandfather, these are not regular binoculars. What are these dials for?"

"All in good time, my child," his Grandfather replied. "Why don't you look at the stars with the binoculars?"

Leon looked up into the night sky with his Grandfather's binoculars. "Grandfather, I can see many stars. They're amazing."

"Turn the first dial and tell me what you see."

"I see a big star, Grandfather," Leon replied. "It's getting bigger now. I see fire and light — bright light."

His Grandfather smiled. "Now, look again, Leon. This time, turn the second dial and tell me what you see."

Leon turned the second dial. "Grandfather, I see spaceships!" he cried out excitedly. He turned to his Grandfather. "But that's impossible!"

"No, Leon, it's not impossible. You have just seen the future. You have seen the Ancestors Yet to Come."

CHECKPOINT

Do you know what Leon's Grandfather means?

Leon looked confused, "I don't understand."

CHECKPOINT

How do the subheadings help you understand the story?

Sky–iStockphoto

Sometime in the past

"Let me tell you a story," his Grandfather said. "Long ago, in the time of our people's ancestors, there lived a great explorer. His name was Lone Wolf. He was called Lone Wolf because he loved to explore and do things on his own. One day, while returning to his Mohawk village, he saw something at the bottom of a tree. It was shining in the afternoon sun. He picked up the strange-looking object, trying to guess what it was. Then, he looked through the eyepieces.

"He turned the first dial and saw the stars. Then, he turned the second dial and saw the future. He saw the spaceships that you saw, Leon. He called them 'sky canoes.' He even saw the people in the sky canoes.

"Lone Wolf was fascinated by the many wonderful things in the sky. Every day, he went back to the same spot where he found the object, and looked into the sky. This went on for many moons.

"One night, while looking with the second dial, Lone Wolf saw a small sky canoe come toward him very fast. It landed not far from where he was standing. An old man got out of the ship and walked toward him. The old man said aloud in the old Mohawk tongue, 'A gift for your family,' as he held out an object that looked exactly like the one Lone Wolf had in his hand. Then the old man quickly walked back to his sky canoe and disappeared.

"Lone Wolf remembered what the old man had said. He knew that what he had was something special. It was a 'gift' for him and his family. He treasured the object and took good care of it. He always

remembered the old man from the sky canoe, and the Ancestors Yet to Come who lived in the spaceships and traveled in the sky canoes. Years later, Lone Wolf gave the object to his son, saying to him, 'Remember this gift from the Ancestors Yet to Come.'"

CHECKPOINT
Can you guess how Lone Wolf was related to Leon Wolf?

Leon's Grandfather then turned to him and said proudly, "Our family has passed the gift from one generation to the next. The gift is now yours, Leon Wolf."

Leon nodded and smiled. "Nia: wen (nee-ah wuhn)," he said in the old Mohawk tongue, which means "Thank you."

Sometime in the future

Wolf was the last of his ancient family. He looked through his work-shop window toward the old home planet, Earth. His family had left Earth long ago, and lived on a new planet among the stars for many years. Many could not remember the home planet, but Wolf did.

Now, as he was nearing the age of 153, Wolf spent much time thinking about the stories of his ancestors. He had cherished the stories, especially the one about Lone Wolf and the gift from the Ancestors Yet to Come. The gift had been passed on, from generation to generation for many years. But it had got lost when the Wolf family traveled to the new planet.

That night, Wolf realized what he had to do. Quickly, he started

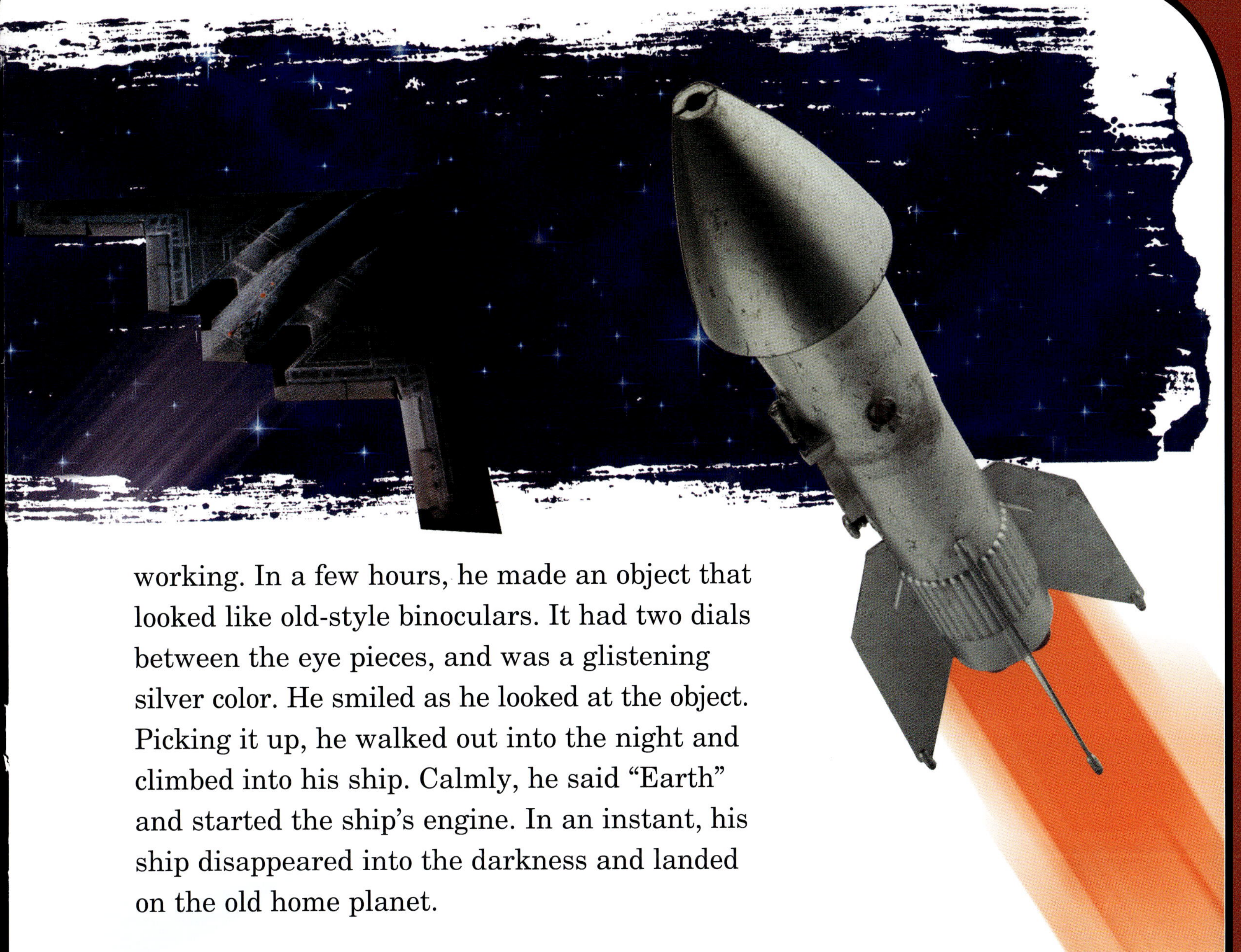

working. In a few hours, he made an object that looked like old-style binoculars. It had two dials between the eye pieces, and was a glistening silver color. He smiled as he looked at the object. Picking it up, he walked out into the night and climbed into his ship. Calmly, he said "Earth" and started the ship's engine. In an instant, his ship disappeared into the darkness and landed on the old home planet.

Wolf stepped out of the ship and walked along a path toward a tree. This is the place, he said to himself. Taking the object out of the bag, he placed it carefully at the bottom of the tree and smiled. He stood up straight and said aloud, in the old Mohawk tongue, "A gift for your family." Then he pointed a short rod at the object and, suddenly, it was gone! He got back into the ship. In a moment, all was silent on the path.

WEB CONNECTIONS

Search for Mohawk Nation on the Internet. Use the information you gather to write a short paragraph about these people.

CHECKPOINT

Pick out instances in the story when the old tongue was used. Why was this?

wrap up

1. Describe the "gift" that Leon Wolf's Grandfather gave him. Why was it special?
2. Imagine you are Lone Wolf telling your story to your son. Use a storyboard to tell how you continue the tradition of passing on the gift.

MILLENNIUM DANCE

All images–iStockphoto

I dreamed alone in the mist of a night,
And heard the Grandfathers call my name.
They told me of a time to come
When Earth would know its galactic fame.

They called in voices ancient and wise
To tell me of our chance:
To call the names of the ancestors
And start the Millennium Dance.

And the voices of time will sing from the skies,
To tell of the age to come
When the Dance will move throughout the land
Holding each and every one.

Slowly at first, the rhythm will move
As life takes a step beyond,
Gathering power and strength in an instant of time
To continue as the day has dawned.

And ancestors will guide as the dance takes shape,
With life together in peace,
And the Millennium will shape around the dance,
From North to South, West to East.

I dreamed alone in the mist of a night,
And heard the Grandfathers call my name.
They told me of the Millennium Dance …

… and nothing would be the same …

By Robert Cutting

warm up

"Millennium" means a thousand years. From reading the title, what would you expect this poem to be about?

FYI

- First Nations people look upon dancing as a very important part of their culture.
- Grandparents have an important place among First Nations people. They are often seen as the keepers of the peoples' stories.
- Ancestors are the people that came before us. They are from the times before our grandparents.

CHECKPOINT

Note the use of sound and movement words in this poem.

wrap up

1. In a short paragraph, describe the story of this poem.
2. Do you think "Millennium Dance" is a good title? Explain why. Suggest two other titles for this poem.
3. Many stories start in our dreams. In a small group, share stories about a special dream.

ACKNOWLEDGMENTS

Every reasonable effort has been made to trace the owners of copyrighted material and to make due acknowledgment. Any errors or omissions drawn to our attention will be gladly rectified in future editions.